Last Wishes

A simple resource guide through the trust process for Grantors, Trustees and Beneficiaries

Susan Arganda Lopez

Susan Arganda Lopez

ISBN: 979-8-2954-4284-1

Disclaimer

Throughout this book, I have shared my personal experiences and insights. I am not a legal professional. The information provided here is based solely on what I have learned from my own journey.

I strongly encourage anyone considering establishing a trust or who has questions about their trust to seek guidance from a qualified legal professional.

Dedication

This book is dedicated to my beautiful parents.

"You fought a good fight, finished the race, and kept the faith" (2 Timothy 4:7).

TABLE OF CONTENTS

Author's Note

Writing an autobiography was never something I anticipated including in this book. My original intent was simply to create a guide, a heartfelt resource to help others navigate a process I came to understand only through personal experience after losing my parents. It has been a journey filled with lessons I never sought and one for which I was wholly unprepared.

To be honest, I never truly imagined life without my parents. They had always been the steady, unshakable center of my world. The thought of their absence was something I never allowed myself to dwell on. Even as they aged, I somehow believed that their presence in my life was permanent; that they would simply always be there.

My parents were, without question, two of the finest people I have ever known. I was blessed with a father whose work ethic and quiet wisdom shaped much of who I am. Though he had little formal education, he possessed a deep hunger for knowledge. He taught himself to read using a single book that became his lifelong companion, the Bible. From him, I learned that wisdom is not confined to classrooms or degrees but grows in the soil of faith and perseverance.

My mother, on the other hand, was grace and warmth embodied. She radiated love—a love that flowed directly from her deep and abiding relationship with Jesus Christ. Together, they formed a partnership rooted in faith, kindness, and integrity. They were my constants, my foundation, my example.

I realize that an autobiography is meant to center on one's own story, but I cannot tell mine without first telling theirs. The truth is, who I am and why this book exists cannot be separated from them. This book was born from loss, the profound loss of both my parents, who passed away from COVID-19 just eleven days apart. Their passing left an immeasurable void, not only in my life but in the hearts of all who loved them. In an instant, life as I knew it was gone. The two pillars that had held me steady were suddenly no more.

My parents' story was one of humble beginnings and enduring devotion. They met as teenagers, married young, raised a family, became loving grandparents, and worked tirelessly to provide for us. Their lives were full of faith, laughter, and purpose, and then all at once, they were gone. The brevity of life revealed itself in the harshest of ways.

I hold tightly to the belief that they are in heaven and that I will see them again one day. That faith brings deep comfort, but it does not erase the ache of their absence. I remember thinking, *Now what?* How do I move forward when my heart feels weighted by grief, sharp, heavy, and unrelenting?

Then came the practical matters, the details no one warns you about. The paperwork and the phone calls that feel so trivial in the shadow of such loss. How could something as sacred as my parents' legacy be reduced to signatures and documents? Even planning a ceremony to celebrate their lives felt almost unbearable. How can lives of eighty-five years each be compressed into a two-hour ceremony? When the service ended, the shock remained. The clock continued to tick forward, unmoved.

In time, the living trust emerged. Suddenly, everything became about who gets what. It was all business, cold and procedural, while my heart was still hurting. I remember praying, *Lord, I need Your supernatural strength, because I cannot do this without You.*

And yet, in an unexpected way, the trust became a bridge back to them. Through it, I felt their presence. The rocks of my life had left stones for me to step on. Their legacy, the fruit of their hard work, became the path that guided me through my grief. Their last wishes were simple: that their children enjoy the blessings they had so lovingly built. Even in loss, I could feel them still watching over me.

I once heard someone say that it is impossible to be both sad and grateful at the same time. I found that gratitude softened the sharp edges of my sorrow.

Of course, the process was not without challenges. Our trust journey came with complications, disagreements among family members, legal setbacks, and long delays.

Throughout this time, many friends and acquaintances have come to me with their own stories of loss and legal confusion. Although I am not a legal expert, I have learned much through experience. It is easy to feel lost when navigating something so complex while grieving. Often, the greatest problems arise from a lack of understanding. Minor misunderstandings can grow into major disputes—issues that might have been avoided if everyone had a clearer sense of what a trust is and the responsibilities it entails.

That realization inspired this book. My purpose in writing it is simple: to offer others a companion through their own journey. I hope to provide insight, comfort, and clarity to help others avoid the unnecessary pitfalls that often accompany this difficult process.

The truth is, no matter how much one prepares, nothing can fully prepare the heart for loss. The process of settling an estate comes with emotion, conflict, and, at times, deep frustration. But whether you find yourself at the beginning, middle, or end of that journey, I hope this guide brings understanding and peace.

Above all, I urge you to remember this: a trust should be honored. Do not allow possessions or paperwork to cloud the memory of the ones you loved. Fulfill their wishes with integrity and love. Their lives mattered, and the way you honor them matters, too.

Page Blank Intentionally

Introduction

Losing a loved one is a deeply emotional and painful experience. Everything changes in an instant. The absence of legal documents such as a will, trust, or power of attorney can create unnecessary stress and confusion during an already difficult time. Navigating legal and financial matters after a death can strain even the strongest family relationships. Family members grieve differently, which often leads to misunderstandings and conflict.

While grief is a personal journey, having legal documents in place can ease the emotional burden that comes with loss. It allows families to grieve properly and to honor their loved one's wishes with peace and clarity.

I am not a legal expert, but I am just someone who has learned a few things along the way through my own journey after the loss of my parents. Since then, many people have reached out to share their own experiences after losing a family member. I'm grateful that I could guide them with what I know, and their stories encouraged me to research the answers I didn't yet have.

The purpose of this guidebook is to help readers begin with the basics:

- ***What is a trust?***
- ***How does it work?***
- ***Provide the Grantor with a guide.***
- ***Remind the Trustee of their duties.***
- ***Inform the beneficiaries of their rights.***
- ***Elder Care Instructions***
- ***Equip readers with the information and tools to make informed decisions.***
- ***What is Probate?***

Closing Thoughts

I hope that this guidebook serves not only as a source of information but also as a companion throughout your journey. May it guide you through the process, help you ask the right questions, avoid common pitfalls, and bring peace of mind to you and to your family. Most of all, may it remind you of the importance of honoring your loved one's memory and their final wishes.

This resource book can serve as a general guide for all states, but keep in mind that the information and interpretation of the 'trust' process explained in this book apply specifically to the State of California. Explicit laws and procedures related to trust administration can vary significantly between states, including property, probate laws, health directives, inheritance, and estate taxes, among other areas.

Ensure Your Last Wishes are Honored

A Simple Resource Guide for Peace of Mind

Are you prepared for the future?

This resource guidebook is your companion for understanding, establishing, and updating your will/trust. Whether you're starting a family, protecting your assets, or ensuring your loved ones are cared for, this guidebook offers clear, step-by-step guidance through the trust process.

Discover the importance of a trust in safeguarding your wishes, avoid common pitfalls, and learn how to make your document legally sound.

You'll find practical advice on:

- Choosing the right Trustee
- Protecting and distributing assets fairly
- Understanding legal requirements and state-specific considerations
- Updating your will/trust as life changes
- Working with estate planning attorneys
- Instructions for Grantor and Families on Elderly Care

I have written this book in simple language. This guidebook will help you act confidently and responsibly, ensuring your legacy is handled just as you intended.

Whether you're writing your first trust or updating an existing one, the *Last Wishes Resource Guidebook* gives you the tools and knowledge you need to take control of your and your family's future today.

Don't leave important decisions to chance. Start planning your legacy now!

What is a Trust?

A trust is a legal document created while someone is alive and dictates how assets will be managed and distributed, both during their lifetime and after their death. It allows for the efficient and private transfer of assets to beneficiaries in accordance with the trust creator's wishes and can also provide for the management of assets in the event of incapacity. It is a tool often used in estate planning to avoid probate and potentially reduce estate taxes.

Key Parties in a Trust

Grantor or Settlor: The individual who creates the trust and transfers assets into it.

Trustee: The person or institution appointed to manage, invest, and distribute the trust assets according to the terms set by the Grantor. The Trustee has a legal duty, known as a fiduciary duty, to act in the best interest of the beneficiaries.

Beneficiary: The individual or group for whom the trust is established and who will ultimately benefit from the trust assets.

Key Features of a Trust

Create the Trust:

You act as the Grantor, Settlor, or creator of the trust, draft a legal document that outlines the terms and conditions of the trust, transferring assets into it while you are living, and then designate a Trustee to manage those assets and distribute them to your chosen beneficiaries upon your death.

Transfer Assets:

You transfer ownership of your assets, such as your home, bank accounts, and investments, into the trust.

Control While You Are Alive:

You typically retain control over the assets in the trust while you are alive and can make changes as needed. You manage the trust assets as Trustee, or you can appoint someone else to do so.

Asset Distribution:

You can specify exactly how and when your assets are distributed to beneficiaries, including real estate, investments, and personal items.

Avoid Probate:

A living trust allows your assets to be transferred directly to beneficiaries quickly and privately, as it bypasses the probate court process in most cases.

Privacy:

Unlike a will, which becomes public record during probate, the terms of a living trust remain private. This privacy can be beneficial for families who prefer to keep their financial matters confidential.

Incapacity Planning:

A living trust can also be used to provide for asset management if you become incapacitated and unable to handle your own finances. The Trustee you appoint can manage your assets to ensure your financial affairs are handled according to your wishes.

Determine the Type of Trust:

Revocable Living Trust or **Irrevocable Living Trust.**

Revocable vs. Irrevocable Trust

The important difference between a revocable trust and an irrevocable trust lies in the Grantor's ability to modify or revoke the trust after it's established. A revocable trust can be changed or terminated by the Grantor during their lifetime, while an irrevocable trust cannot be altered or revoked except in rare circumstances and with the consent of the beneficiaries.

Revocable Trust:

A Revocable Living Trust can be changed or terminated at any time

Flexibility:

The Grantor retains control and can make changes, add or remove assets or the terms of distribution, modify beneficiaries and Trustees, or even terminate the trust at any time during their lifetime as long as they have the mental capacity to do so.

Control:

The Grantor maintains ownership and control over the trust assets and how they are managed during their lifetime. Trusts allow the Grantor to dictate exactly when and how their assets are distributed, which is especially useful for minors, those with special needs, or beneficiaries who are not prepared to manage large sums.

Tax Implications:

Assets held in a revocable trust are generally included in the Grantor's estate and subject to estate taxes upon death.

Asset or Credit Protection:

Revocable Trusts do not provide significant protection from creditors or lawsuits while the Grantor is alive.

Irrevocable Trust:

An Irrevocable Trust **cannot be changed** once it's established, but it creates a complete legal separation between the Grantor and their assets, and the assets are shielded from legal claims.

Asset Protection:

Offers a level of security protecting your assets from lawsuits, creditors, and unexpected financial challenges.

Tax Advantages:

Assets are typically excluded from the Grantor's taxable estate, potentially reducing or eliminating estate taxes.

Gift Tax Planning:

Gifting a home to children will have fewer tax implications.

Control and Flexibility:

While the Grantor relinquishes direct control over the assets, they specify how and when beneficiaries receive distributions through the trust document.

Privacy:

The terms of an Irrevocable Trust are generally not made public, unlike those of a will, which become part of the public record.

Medicaid Planning:

Eligibility for government benefits. In some cases, Irrevocable Trusts can be used to help individuals become eligible for Medicaid or other government benefits by reducing countable assets.

Expert Advise

As with all significant financial decisions, it's essential to consult with qualified legal and tax professionals to ensure that the trust complies with relevant laws, accurately reflects the Grantors' wishes, includes the correct provisions and verbiage, and minimizes the potential for future disputes or misinterpretations.

Closing Thoughts

Revocable Trust: It is a flexible tool for estate planning, allowing for ongoing adjustments and control.

Irrevocable Trust: It is more of a permanent arrangement, offering potential tax advantages and asset protection from creditors, and provides for future generations, at the cost of flexibility.

They both offer greater protection than a will and avoid probate.

What is a Will?

A Will, also known as a ***"Last Will and Testament"***, is a written, legally binding document in which a person specifies how their assets and possessions should be managed and distributed upon their death. It allows individuals to express their wishes regarding the distribution of their property, care of their minor children, and the administration of their estate after their death.

A will ensures your wishes are respected and helps avoid potential conflicts among family members regarding your possessions. It also provides clarity on how your affairs should be handled, including funeral arrangements and final bills.

What Assets Can I Put in a Will?

You can place most of your assets into a will:

- ***Real Estate***
- ***Bank Accounts***
- ***Vehicles***
- ***Investments like Stocks and Bonds***
- ***Business Interests***
- ***Personal belongings such as jewelry and furniture***
- ***Pets***

What Happens Without a Will?

When an individual dies without a will, the Intestate laws dictate how the estate is divided, which may not align with the deceased's wishes. This can lead to unintended consequences, prolonged legal processes, and potential disputes among surviving heirs.

If I Have a Will, Do I Avoid Probate?

No, having a will does not guarantee you will avoid probate; in fact, it often requires probate to validate the will and distribute assets legally, unless all assets are held in a way that bypasses probate, such as a living trust, joint ownership, or named beneficiaries. A will instructs the court on how to distribute your assets, but the probate court still needs to oversee the process to confirm the will's validity and ensure debts are paid.

Trust vs. Will

A will distributes your assets after you die, but it must go through a public, potentially lengthy probate process. A trust is a legal arrangement that can take effect while you're alive, manage and distribute your assets through a private, more efficient process, and can be especially useful for protecting beneficiaries or providing for their ongoing needs. While wills are simpler and essential for naming guardians, trusts offer more control and privacy for your assets after death.

Do I still need a Will if I have a Trust?

Yes, even if you have a trust, most estate plans include what's called a "**pour-over will**" that acts as a safety net for your estate, ensuring that any assets not transferred into the trust during your lifetime are still included in your overall estate planning. It allows you to name guardians for minor children and specify other wishes not covered by the trust. Without it, those assets would go through probate and be distributed according to state law, which may not match your wishes. Having a trust and a will makes for a more complete, flexible, and reliable estate.

Closing Thoughts

While a trust is a powerful estate planning tool, it is not a complete replacement for a will. Most people should have both a trust to manage and distribute major assets and a will to cover anything else and serve as a backup. Consulting with an estate planning attorney can help ensure your wishes are fully protected and your loved ones are provided for according to your intentions.

What is Probate?

Probate is the legal, court-supervised process that handles matters related to a person's estate after they die. The probate court's main job is to make sure the person's property, debts, and final wishes are handled legally and fairly.

What the Probate Court usually does:

- Validates a will (if there is one)
- Appoints an executor or administrator to manage the estate
- Oversees payment of debts and taxes
- Supervises the distribution of property and assets to rightful heirs or beneficiaries
- Handles disputes about the will or inheritance

If There is a Will

The court determines whether the will is valid and, if so, usually authorizes the named executor to carry out the instructions.

If There is No Will

The court appoints someone to manage the estate, and state law decides who inherits

Does every Estate go through probate?

Not always. Some assets can pass directly to others without probate, such as:

- Life Insurance with named beneficiaries
- Retirement and pension accounts with named beneficiaries
- Jointly owned property
- Assets in a living trust

Four Main Reasons to Avoid Probate

- **High financial costs:** Probate fees can drain 3% to 7% of the estate's total value. Families must pay court costs, filing fees, executor fees, and mandatory attorney fees before heirs receive anything.
- **Extensive time delays:** The process routinely takes 1 to 3 years to complete, sometimes longer. During this time, family assets are often frozen, making it difficult for survivors to pay for immediate living expenses or funeral costs.
- **Increased risk of family disputes:** The public court setting makes it much easier for disgruntled relatives to contest their will. This frequently leads to bitter litigation and permanently damaged family relationships.
- The probate court system is not completely immune to illegal influences. It can involve bad actors who find their way to excessively bill and purposely delay. Because significant sums of money and property are involved, it can create opportunities for misconduct and fraudulent practices among legal professionals in the court system.

How to Avoid Probate

To avoid probate, you must arrange your assets so they transfer automatically to your heirs upon your death without requiring court intervention. This specific strategy depends on the types of assets you own.

- Transfer ownership of your assets into a revocable or irrevocable trust.
- Add beneficiary designations into certain accounts, which allow you to name a direct recipient, which overrides any instructions left in a standard will, such as:
  - **Payable on Death (POD)** designation to your checking, savings, and CDs.
    (see page 33).

- **Transfer on Death (TOD)**. You register your stocks, bonds, or brokerage accounts. (see page 33).
- **Retirement and Life Insurance Beneficiaries**. Complete beneficiary forms directly with your provider for 404 (k)s, IRA's, and life insurance policies.
- **Establish Joint Ownership of Property**. Owning property jointly with someone else can ensure an automatic transfer of real estate or vehicles. When one owner dies, their share automatically transfers to the surviving owner(s) without court involvement.

Three Core Parties That Make Up a Trust

- The **Grantor** creates the plan.
- The **Trustee** administers the trust.
- The **Beneficiary** receives the benefits.

Together, they make a living trust useful for:

- Avoiding probate.
- Planning for incapacity.
- Managing assets privately
- Distributing property efficiently

The following pages, 13-32, explain the importance of each of the roles and responsibilities.

To the Grantor…

Your last wishes in a trust are more than just legal instructions—they are a final, heartfelt expression of love, your values, and your vision for your family's future. By creating this document, you are continuing to care for your loved ones even after you're gone. It's your way of saying, "I've got you covered. I handled the complicated part so you can focus on healing."

Grantor

A Grantor, also called the Settlor, is the person who creates the trust and transfers assets into it. They set the rules for how the trust's assets will be managed and distributed and identify their beneficiaries. The Grantor chooses a trustee to manage the trust's assets according to the trust agreement.

Grantor's Checklist

This checklist is designed to guide and help the Grantor create, maintain, and maximize the benefits of the trust.

1. **Choose the Type of Trust**
    - Individual or Joint Trust: Decide if you want a single Trust for one person or a Joint Trust, typically for married couples.
    - Revocable or Irrevocable Trust

2. **Identify and List All Trust Assets**

Make a thorough inventory of all assets you want to transfer into the trust:

- Real Estate – homes, vacation properties, and land.
- Bank Accounts – checking, savings, CDs, money market.
- Investment Accounts – stocks, bonds, mutual funds, retirement accounts.
- Personal Property – vehicles, jewelry, art, collectibles.
- Business Interests.
- Life Insurance Policies (if you want the trust to be the beneficiary or owner).
- Other Valuables.

3. **Select a Trustee**

    - Appoint yourself as the initial Trustee (common for revocable trusts), with the right to manage and control assets.
    - Designate a successor trustee to step in upon your incapacity or death.
    - Carefully choose someone who is reliable, trustworthy, financially astute, and aligned with your family's needs.
    - Ensure the Trustee can fulfill their fiduciary duties and act in the best interest of the beneficiaries.
    - For larger or more complex trusts, it is highly recommended to get an experienced estate planning attorney to manage the assets effectively. For smaller trusts, a family member or friend is usually named.

4. **Name Your Beneficiaries**

    - Clearly identify who will receive trust assets after your death – it can be individuals like spouses, children, other family members, friends, or entities.
    - Include contingent beneficiaries in case your primary beneficiaries predecease you.
    - Consider the use of sub-trusts if you have minors, special needs dependents, or want to control distributions over time.

5. **Draft Trust Document**

    - Work with a qualified estate planning attorney to draft the trust document according to your wishes and relevant laws.
    - Name the trust document.
    - Assess your financial situation and family structure, and outline the terms of the trust.

- Review the document carefully to ensure all details and instructions are accurate and comprehensive.
- Sign the trust document in the presence of a notary public.
- Retain original signed copies in a safe and accessible location.

6. Fund the Trust

Legally transfer ownership of each asset into the name of the trust:

- Transfer property into the trust by drafting a new deed that transfers ownership from the Grantors' names to the trust's name.
- After you have transferred the property into the trust, notify your homeowners insurance company so that they can add the trust as an "additional insured" to avoid claim denials or coverage gaps.
- Changing account ownership at financial institutions is not mandatory but recommended.
- Transfer titles for vehicles.
- Assign personal property using a written assignment.

Confirm with banks, brokerage firms, insurance companies, and other custodians about their requirements for changing ownership or beneficiary designations. Keep records of all transfers and confirmations.

What Cannot Be Placed into a Trust?

You cannot place certain assets in a trust due to legal, tax, or practical reasons, including retirement accounts like IRAs, 401 (k)s, health savings accounts, assets held in a foreign country, and potentially vehicles. These must remain in your own name.

7. **Prepare for Incapacity**

    - Set up provisions in your trust for the management of assets if you become incapacitated.
    - The trust document should clearly define what constitutes incapacity, often requiring confirmation from a medical professional.
    - The plan should allow for a seamless return of management to the Grantor if they recover their mental capacity, especially for temporary incapacities due to illness or injury.
    - Make sure your successor trustee understands their duties and has access to the necessary documents and contacts.
    - Consider combining the trust with powers of attorney for a comprehensive incapacity plan.

8. **Coordinate Trust with Your Estate Plan**

Ensure your trust works in harmony with your estate planning documents, such as:

- Last Will and Testament.
- Durable Power of Attorney (for finances).
- Advance Healthcare Directives/Living Will.
- Beneficiary designations on retirement accounts and insurance policies.

9. **Communicate with Your Family and Advisors**

It is beneficial for a grantor to communicate with family about the trust to prevent future conflicts, ensure expectations are understood, and provide clarity on their wishes, though the decision depends on family dynamics and personal comfort with transparency.

- Let your successor trustee and key beneficiaries know about the trust and where to find important documents.

- Share contact information for your attorney, accountant, and financial advisor with those who may need it.

10. Review Tax Implications

- Understand the potential tax consequences of transferring assets to the trust and any ongoing tax responsibilities.
- Consult with a tax professional regarding federal and state estate, gift, and income tax considerations.
- Ensure your trust is structured to minimize tax liability where possible.

11. Update and Maintain Your Trust

- Periodically review your trust to ensure it reflects your current wishes, assets, and family situation.
- Amend the trust as necessary to account for changes in relationships, asset ownership, or beneficiary designations.
- Continue to add new assets to the trust as you acquire them and keep an updated inventory and records of all assets held by the trust.
- Keep an updated inventory and records of all assets held by the trust.

12. Periodic Check-Ups

- Revisit your living trust at least every few years or after major life events like marriage, divorce, birth, death, acquisition, or sale of significant assets.
- Stay informed about changes in laws that may affect your trust or estate plan.
- Meet with your attorney/financial advisor regularly to keep your plan up to date.

13. Store and Protect Your Documents

- Keep your signed trust document in a safe, fireproof location.
- Provide copies to your trustees, attorney, and trusted individuals, as appropriate.
- Maintain an easily accessible list of trust assets and account numbers.
- Ensure someone you trust knows how to access these documents in case of an emergency.

Closing Thoughts

Creating and managing a living trust is a proactive step toward protecting your legacy and providing for your loved ones. This checklist is intended to ensure that your living trust is properly established, funded, and maintained, giving you peace of mind that your wishes will be honored now and in the future. Always seek professional legal and financial advice customized to your unique situation before making or changing your trust arrangements.

To the Trustee…

You hold a special position of honor in preserving the Grantor's legacy. Your role may be challenging at times, but a solid understanding of your fiduciary duties will help you navigate obstacles and prevent problems. Remember, you are legally required to maintain accurate records. This ensures transparency, protects everyone involved, and keeps the process fair. If things ever become too complex, seek legal guidance to help you stay on course.

Trustee

A trustee is an individual who is legally responsible for managing and administering assets held in a trust according to the terms of the trust document and applicable laws, always acting in the best interest of the beneficiaries.

Duties of a Trustee

Fiduciary Duty

Trustees have a legal and ethical obligation to act in the best interest of the beneficiaries. They have a duty to act with honesty, impartiality, and good faith, avoiding conflicts of interest and managing and preserving the trust's assets prudently, and avoiding any actions that could cause financial harm to the trust. Breach of fiduciary duty may result in legal consequences, including removal from office, restitution, and potential civil liability.

- **Duty of Loyalty** – A Trustee must always place the interests of the beneficiaries above their own. They must avoid conflicts of interest and refrain from self-dealing, which means not using trust assets for personal gain. And trustees cannot commingle trust assets with personal assets.
- **Duty of Impartiality** – When there are multiple beneficiaries, the Trustee must act fairly and impartially, considering the interests of each without favor or prejudice.
- **Duty of Prudence** – Trustees are expected to manage the trust's assets with care, skill, and diligence that a prudent person would exercise. They should make informed decisions, seek professional advice when necessary, and avoid unnecessary risk.
- **Duty to Act in Accordance with the Trust Instrument** – Trustees are bound by the instructions and limitations set in the trust document. They must respect the Grantor's intentions and act within the scope granted by the trust.

Administrative Duties

- **Asset Management** – Trustees must protect the trust property. This includes securing physical assets, managing investments, and safeguarding financial accounts.
- **Record Keeping and Accounting** – Accurate and timely records must be maintained, documenting all transactions, receipts, disbursements, and correspondence. Trustees are often required to prepare regular financial statements and reports for beneficiaries.
- **Investments** – Trustees are generally expected to invest trust assets productively, suited to the trust objectives and beneficiaries' needs.
- **Tax Compliance** – Trustees must ensure that all tax filings relating to the trust are completed promptly and accurately, including income, capital gains, and estate taxes. They may need to consult with tax professionals to fulfill these obligations.
- **Distribution of Assets** – Trustees are responsible for distributing income to beneficiaries in a timely manner. They must interpret the trust document to ensure distributions are made properly.

Communication Duties

- **Duty to Inform and Report** – Trustees must provide beneficiaries with information about the trust, its assets, and its administration. This often includes annual reports, statements, and updates regarding major decisions.
- **Responding to Requests** – Trustees should respond to reasonable requests for information from beneficiaries in a timely and thorough manner and be transparent regarding the trust's administration. Withholding information or providing misleading statements is strictly prohibited.
- **Consultation and Engagement** – In some situations, trustees

may need to consult beneficiaries on important decisions, particularly those that materially affect their interests.

Legal and Ethical Responsibilities

- **Compliance With the Law** – Trustees must act in accordance with all applicable laws, including trust law, tax law, security regulations, and anti-money laundering rules.
- **Seeking Professional Advice** – When faced with complex issues, trustees should seek professional assistance from lawyers, accountants, financial advisors, or other experts. Ignorance of technical matters is not an excuse for mismanagement.
- **Avoiding Delegation of Core Duties** – While Trustees may delegate certain tasks, they cannot delegate their ultimate decision-making authority or overall responsibility for the trust.
- **Safeguarding Confidentiality** – Trustees must protect the privacy and confidentiality of beneficiaries and trust affairs. Disclosure of sensitive information is only permitted where required by law or with proper authorization.

Potential Liabilities and Remedies

Trustees who breach their duties may be held personally liable for losses to the trust or for improper conduct.

- **Surcharges and Damages:** Courts may impose surcharges requiring trustees to compensate for losses resulting from negligence or misconduct.
- **Removal and Replacement:** If a trustee acts improperly, beneficiaries or courts may seek their removal and the appointment of a new trustee.
- **Restitution:** Trustees may be ordered to return any benefits gained through improper conduct or self-dealing.

Closing Thoughts

The role of the Trustee is vital and demands a high degree of integrity, requiring a blend of legal knowledge, financial expertise, and ethical judgment. The duties of a trustee extend far beyond mere asset management; they encompass the faithful stewardship of property, adherence to instructions, transparent communication, and the unwavering protection of beneficiary interests.

Whether overseeing a modest family trust or a more complex trust, trustees must approach their responsibilities with dedication, impartiality, and professionalism, adhering to their duties so that they can faithfully execute the intentions of the trust's creator and secure the trust's legacy for present and future generations.

Trustee Checklist

1. **Locate and Review the Trust Agreement**

Thoroughly read and understand the terms of the trust, including the Grantor's intentions and the powers and responsibilities of the Trustee.

2. **Prepare an Affidavit of Death of Trust**

This is a legal document that the successor trustee files with the county recorder to officially record the death of the previous Trustee and to transfer property held in the trust.

3. **Acceptance of Trusteeship**

This is a document the successor trustee signs to confirm they accept their nomination to manage the trust.

4. **Consult with Professionals**

If a trustee finds a trust too complex to manage, they should seek professional guidance from an experienced trust and estate lawyer to ensure they fulfill their duties ethically and diligently.

5. **Notify Beneficiaries**

Trustees have a legal duty to formally notify beneficiaries that they are included in a trust, and they must do so within a specific time frame, including providing a copy of the trust.

6. **Request Death Certificates**

- Request original certified copies of the death certificate from the Grantor's residing County Recorder's Office.
- Provide certificates to organizations and institutions for various purposes, such as settling estates, claiming benefits, or closing accounts.

7. Obtain a Date of Death Appraisal on Properties

Trustees are not legally required to obtain a date-of-death appraisal, but it is highly recommended to determine fair market value and for proper trust administration, tax purposes, and asset distribution.

8. Transfer Bank Accounts to Trust

The Trustee will need to close the Grantor's existing account and open a new trust account under the name of the trust to manage trust assets.

9. Identify and Value Trust Assets

- Create a detailed inventory of all trust assets, including real estate, bank accounts, life insurance policies, investments, and personal property.
- Conduct a complete inventory of all items in and on the property, such as furniture, jewelry, family heirlooms, automobiles, etc.

10. Sell or Transfer Property

Before the Sale

- Review and understand the terms of the trust, including any specific instructions regarding property sales.
- Obtain a professional appraisal.
- Inform all beneficiaries and creditors about the intended sale.
- Ensure all debts and outstanding obligations are addressed.
- Gather all necessary and relevant documents, including the trust document, deeds, and other necessary paperwork.

During the Sale

- List the property for sale and market it appropriately.
- Secure a qualified buyer.
- Provide regular updates to beneficiaries about the progress of the

sale.

After the Sale

- Use the sale proceeds to pay any outstanding debts, taxes, and expenses related to the property sale.
- Prepare a final accounting of the trust's finances, including the sale of the property.
- Distribute any remaining assets according to the trust document.
- Maintain accurate records of all transactions related to the sale and provide beneficiaries with copies of any sale-related documents to ensure transparency and accountability.

10. Keep Beneficiaries Informed

- Regularly communicate with beneficiaries about the trust's administration, including the status of assets, distributions, and any significant events.
- Provide regular accounting to beneficiaries, detailing the trust income, expenses, and distributions.

11. Pay Debts and Taxes

- Pay any outstanding debts and liabilities of the trust.
- File the decedent's final federal and state income tax returns.
- Pay any taxes that may be due, including estate taxes.

12. Distribute Assets

- Distribute the trust assets to the beneficiaries according to the terms of the trust.
- Follow any specific instructions in the trust regarding distribution timelines and methods.

13. Close the Trust

Once all assets have been distributed and all debts and taxes have been paid, the trust can be closed. File any necessary paperwork with the appropriate authorities and provide all final accounting to the beneficiaries.

Trustee Entitlement

Far too often, some trustees can and do feel entitled, which can lead to conflicts and legal problems. A trustee's role is a position of fiduciary trust, meaning they are legally and ethically obligated to act in the best interest of the beneficiaries, not themselves.

When a trustee's personal interest overrides their duties, it is considered a breach of fiduciary duty. This sense of entitlement is most likely to develop in family members who are appointed as trustees and have a pre-existing relationship with the trust creator and beneficiaries.

Factors That Lead to a Trustee Feeling Entitled

- **The Emotional Toll of the Role:** The responsibility of managing a trust can be a "thankless job", leading some trustees to resent their duties, especially if they are also grieving the trust creator.
- **Lack of Understanding of Fiduciary Duty:** Some family members, particularly if they are not legal or financial professionals, may not fully grasp the high standard of care required of them. They may mistakenly believe their personal efforts in managing the trust justify extraordinary compensation or a disproportionate share of the assets.
- **A Trustee Who is Also a Beneficiary:** While it is legal for a trustee to be a beneficiary, it creates a conflict of interest that requires careful management. A trustee/beneficiary who prioritizes their own distributions over other beneficiaries is engaging in self-dealing.
- **Vague or Conflicting Trust Documents:** If the trust document is not specific about compensation or the timing of distribution, a trustee may interpret the terms to their own benefit, especially if beneficiaries are not well informed of their rights.

- **Pre-existing Family Conflicts:** Historical issues and resentments can be magnified during the stress of trust administration. An entitled trustee may leverage their position to punish a sibling or other beneficiaries over past grievances.

Signs of an Entitled Trustee

Excessive Compensation: Taking more than the reasonable compensation allowed by law, especially when the trust does not specify the fee amount.

Self-dealing: Engaging in transactions that primarily benefit themselves, such as selling trust property to themselves at below market rates, using trust assets for personal gain, or paying themselves exorbitant fees.

Withholding Information: Refusing to provide accountings or copies of the trust document to beneficiaries.

Biased Distributions: Making discretionary distributions that favor themselves or a preferred beneficiary over others.

Mismanagement of Assets: Making high-risk investments for personal benefit or simply acting negligently with trust property.

Recourse for Beneficiaries

Beneficiaries are not powerless if a trustee acts with a sense of entitlement.

They have the right to challenge a trustee's actions by:

- Demanding a formal accounting.
- Requesting the removal of the Trustee by filing a petition with the probate court.
- Suing for the recovery of misappropriated funds.

To the Beneficiary…

The Grantor had you in mind when they created their trust. Seeing your inheritance as part of the Grantor's legacy can help you find meaning and honor their memory. Take the time to read the trust carefully and understand its terms. Stay informed, know your rights, and keep communication open with the Trustee. You are entitled to full transparency; the trust was created for you.

Beneficiary

Legal Protections and Privileges of Trust Beneficiaries

A beneficiary of a trust is a person or entity for whom the trust was created. They are named in a trust document and entitled to receive benefits from the trust, such as income or assets, according to the terms outlined in the trust document.

The rights of beneficiaries are critical to ensure that the trust functions as intended and that their interests are protected throughout the lifecycle of the trust.

The relationship between the Trustee and beneficiaries is fiduciary in nature, imposing the highest standard of care and loyalty from the Trustee.

Beneficiaries Rights

1. **Right to Information and Disclosure**

   - **Access to Trust Documents:** Beneficiaries are generally entitled to reasonable access to the trust instrument, amendments, and related documents. This allows them to understand the nature of their interest and the trustees' duties.

   - **Accounting and Reporting:** Beneficiaries have the right to periodic accountings of trust assets, income, expenses, and distributions. Trustees must provide accurate, up-to-date records and notify beneficiaries of significant transactions or changes.

   - **Transparency:** Trustees must keep beneficiaries reasonably informed about the trust administration and material facts necessary for the protection of their interests.

2. Right to Fair and Impartial Administration

- **Impartiality:** Trustees are legally obligated to treat all beneficiaries fairly and impartially. This means no beneficiary's interest should be favored or prejudiced without clear authorization.
- **Prudent Management:** Trustees must manage trust assets with reasonable care, skill, and caution, investing and protecting assets in the beneficiary's best interest.

3. Right to Proper Distribution of Income in Principle

- **Timely Distributions:** Beneficiaries are entitled to receive distributions of income as prescribed by the trust instrument. Trustees may not unreasonably delay or withhold distributions without cause.
- **Compliance With Trust Terms:** Trustees must follow the trust's instructions regarding who receives distributions, how much, and when. If discretionary powers are granted, trustees must exercise them in good faith and for a proper purpose.

4. Right to Enforce the Terms of the Trust

- **Legal Standing:** Beneficiaries have the right to initiate legal process meetings to enforce the terms of the trust, compel the Trustee to perform their duties, or challenge improper actions.
- **Remedies for Breach:** If a trustee breaches their fiduciary duty or the terms of the trust, beneficiaries may seek court intervention, including removal of the Trustee, recovery of losses, or other equitable relief.

5. Right to Remove or Replace a Trustee

Beneficiaries can petition the court to remove a trustee for cause, such as mismanagement, self-dealing, incompetence, or failure to act. The court may appoint a new trustee to safeguard the beneficiary's interest.

6. **Right to Protection from Trustee Misconduct**

- **Fiduciary Duty:** Trustees owe beneficiaries duties of loyalty, prudence, and impartiality. Any action contrary to these duties exposes the Trustee to potential liability.

- **Remedies for Misconduct:** Courts can order trustees to make beneficiaries whole, return misappropriated assets, or take other actions to restore trust integrity.

Enforcement of Rights and Remedies

Beneficiaries who believe their rights have been violated should act promptly.

Steps may include:

- Requesting information or clarification from the Trustee in writing.

- Consulting with a qualified attorney specializing in trust law.

- Filing a petition in probate or civil court to compel action or seek remedies for breach.

Courts possess broad authority to enforce trust terms, remove trustees, order restitution, and mold equitable solutions to protect beneficiary interests.

Practical Tips for Beneficiaries

- Maintain open communications with the Trustee and keep records of all correspondence.

- Review trust documents carefully and understand the terms of your beneficial interest.

- Seek periodic accounting and clarify many unclear transactions or distributions.

- If concerns arise, address them quickly to avoid the loss of rights through delay or inaction.

- Consider mediation or alternative dispute resolution before resorting to litigation, if possible.

Closing Thoughts

The rights of beneficiaries are essential to the proper functioning of the trust relationship and serve as important checks on trustee power. While specific rights may differ based on the trust instrument, beneficiaries are generally entitled to information, fair treatment, proper distributions, and legal recourse. Understanding these rights and powers enables beneficiaries to protect their interest and ensure the faithful administration of trust assets for the current and future generations.

Other Essential Estate Planning Documents

POD (Payable on Death) and TOD (Transfer on Death)

A **Payable on Death (POD) form** and a **Transfer on Death (TOD) form**, also known as a beneficiary designation, are legal document that allows you to designate a beneficiary to inherit your bank and investment accounts after your death, bypassing the probate process.

This means that the beneficiary can access the funds directly and can only access them upon the account holder's death; the account holder maintains full control of the accounts during their lifetime. POD and TODs are established by completing a simple form with the account holder's bank. If this is not completed, funds go through probate upon the account holder's death.

Durable Power of Attorney (POA) for Financial Decisions

This document allows someone you trust (called the agent) to manage your financial and legal matters on your behalf if you become incapacitated. This is crucial for potential future incapacitation due to illness, accidents, or unforeseen circumstances. It can be broader than the limited power of attorney, ensuring your finances are managed without court intervention.

Medical Power of Attorney

This is also called **Healthcare Power of Attorney**. It allows your agent to make healthcare decisions if you are unable to communicate them yourself and allows your agent to make decisions regarding medical treatments, procedures, medications, and even end-of-life care.

Advance Health Directive (Living Will)

This document specifies what type of life-sustaining medical treatments you do or do not want, such as resuscitation, ventilation, feeding tubes, or dialysis, in the event of permanent unconsciousness or terminal illness. It provides clear instructions and helps prevent possible disputes among relatives.

HIPAA Authorization

This document allows your designated healthcare agents to speak to healthcare providers and access your medical information.

Guardianship Documents

If you have minor children or dependents with special needs, it's crucial to designate a guardian. This ensures that someone you trust will care for them if anything happens to you. This can be done through a will or through a separate guardianship document.

Closing Thoughts

A **will** and a **trust** only control what happens to your property when you die, while these essential documents protect you, your dignity, and personal choices during a medical or legal crisis while you are alive.

Common Scenarios

The Daughter-In-Law Receives The Inheritance That Was Intended For The Son And Grandchildren

This can happen, even when the Grantor says, ***"I want everything to go to my children, and if they predecease me, I want it to then go to their children, the grandchildren."***

Often, it ends up in the hands of the son's wife. Most likely, the son will survive the Grantor, and when the Grantor passes, the trust terminates. The inheritance usually ends up getting commingled with the spouse, and then if the son passes away, the grandkids get disinherited even though they were named in the trust.

The proper trust language needs to be strong enough to protect the grandchildren's inheritance. When meeting with a lawyer, the Grantor's intentions must be clearly stated in the trust document to ensure the inheritance reaches the intended beneficiaries.

A **Bloodline Trust**, or a similar trust structure, can protect the inheritance from being subject to equitable distribution if the son gets divorced or dies, ensuring it remains within the family bloodline.

Trust Was Never Updated or Amended, and the Trustee Takes Over

The Grantor created a trust and listed his sister as Trustee and his minor children as beneficiaries. After establishing the trust, he started a new business and purchased additional property.

He became estranged from his sister but never amended his trust to remove her as Trustee or transfer his property and business into the trust. Years later, he passed away. The sister, with whom he had been estranged, assumed the role of Trustee and immediately took over his property and all his assets, and excluded his now-grown children and other close family members from receiving anything. The children hired a lawyer and are fighting to reclaim their rightful inheritance.

It is important to understand the consequences of not updating your trust document and adding new assets after major life changes. Any assets that are acquired after a trust is established will not automatically become part of the trust unless the title to the property is formally transferred into the trust's name. In this case, **Intestacy Laws** could come into play. If assets are not included in the trust, those assets could be distributed according to the laws of intestate succession. This means assets could be distributed to the closest living relatives in a specific order defined by state law, most likely the children.

If the Trustee takes possession of trust assets without being a beneficiary and does so for her own benefit, this is a breach of fiduciary duty and likely theft or embezzlement, leading to removal from her position and liability for financial losses and possible criminal charges.

A Son is Told That His Mother Left No Will or Trust, and the Granddaughter Assumed All Assets

An elderly woman owned a home and other assets. She had four children. Three of the children had passed away, and her only surviving son lived out of state. One of her granddaughters lived with her for two years and became her caregiver when the woman could no longer care for herself.

The son would occasionally visit, but never talked to his mom about any final preparations. After she died, the granddaughter told the son that his mom left no will or trust and informed him that she was going to continue to live in the home. The son had no idea what to do or what his rights were, and never inquired to find out if he was entitled to anything.

The son could have checked with the county probate court in the county where his mother resided to see if a will or trust was ever established. Every state is different, but in California, if an elderly person dies without a will or trust, their house and assets will be distributed according to the state's **Intestate Succession Laws**. The house would have gone to the son as the primary beneficiary in the absence of a will or spouse. The granddaughter would generally only inherit anything if the surviving son was not alive to receive his share.

An Aging Parent was Pressured to Modify Her Living Trust

An elderly woman, recently widowed and suffering from declining health, is persuaded by her oldest son to rewrite her living trust, leaving most of her estate to him.

The trust originally listed all four of her children as beneficiaries to receive equal shares. The son tried to convince her that his dad would have wanted him to receive more since he was the only son. He used emotional appeals, intimidation tactics, and misinformation to sway his mom's decision. After intense pressure, the mother agreed to change the terms of the trust. The other three children found out what their brother did and challenged the modifications in court, alleging undue influence.

An undue influence is sadly common in situations involving elderly people where they are manipulated by family members, caregivers, or others. Vulnerable individuals may be pressured into signing documents, changing wills, or making financial decisions that favor the influencer.

At no time can anyone use excessive persuasion to overcome someone else's free will to benefit themselves. In this case, the court finds evidence of isolation, secrecy, and the sons' active involvement in the modification of the trust. The court set aside the modification and restored the original trust terms. The son was disinherited, and the court ordered him to pay legal fees to the estate and other beneficiaries.

Closing Thoughts

- It is very important that the trust language and provisions be clear and unambiguous to ensure the trust creator's intentions are carried out, prevent misunderstandings, and avoid costly legal disputes among beneficiaries and trustees. Vague or unclear terms can lead to family conflict, failed financial goals, and court intervention to interpret or modify the trust.

- You should regularly renew and update your trust because life circumstances, family situations, and the law change over time.
- It is critically important for beneficiaries to know their rights. Being well-informed empowers them to ensure the trust is administered properly and that their inheritance is protected. A lack of knowledge can make beneficiaries vulnerable to mismanagement, unfair treatment, and delays.
- Undue influence is prohibited.

It is important for key individuals in a trust – namely, **the Grantor**, **Trustee**, and **beneficiaries** – to obtain legal counsel to ensure the trust is created properly, administered according to the law, and that their respective interests are protected.

A lawyer can help navigate complex laws, prevent missteps, protect assets, and resolve disputes, ensuring the trust functions effectively and as intended.

Elder Care Planning

"My goal is to live my life on my own terms and remain in control of my decisions for as long as I am able. My trust and estate plan are designed to support my independence, not take it away".

While a living trust manages and distributes your assets after you pass, incorporating advanced care planning ensures your health care wishes are honored and your assets are protected if you become incapacitated during your lifetime.

No one ever plans to be sick or disabled. Yet, planning can make all the difference in an emergency and at the end of life. Being prepared and having important documents in a single place can give you Peace of Mind, help ensure your wishes are honored, and ease the burden on your loved ones. Plan for where and how you want to live as your needs change and identify who can help, whether that's family, friends, or professional caregivers.

If you suffer a sudden medical emergency without a legal plan in place, a court may have to step in and appoint a conservator or guardian to make decisions regarding your care and estate. This process takes away your choice of who manages your life finances and places the burden on your family to navigate a very complex legal system.

As discussed in this resource guide, essential tools for aging and advanced care include:

- **Advanced Healthcare Directives**
- **Healthcare Power of Attorney**
- **Financial Power of Attorney Long-Term Care Strategies**

(Refer to the "Other Essential Documents" page for more information).

- **Explore Care Options**
- **Discuss Your Wishes with Your Spouse, Children, and Close Friends**
- **Review Financial Preparations**
- **Age-In-Place Plan to Make Arrangements to Live Safely at Home**

Because these legal and medical choices work hand in hand, understanding how to structure your estate strategy with long-term care in mind is essential.

Information and Plan to Care for Aging Parents

"To care for those who once cared for us is one of the highest honors"

Care Giving

Caring for aging parents can be incredibly rewarding, but it is a challenging period and forces an adult child to navigate a complex role reversal, often while balancing their own career, personal life, or family. This transition can bring significant emotional, physical, and financial strains.

Emotional Strain and Grief: Watching a parent's health decline causes anticipatory grief. The parent-child relationship fundamentally changes. Caregivers frequently deal with role reversals, feeling more like a parent to their own mother or father, which can be psychologically difficult.

Slow Transition: Families rarely make a formal care plan. The transition usually begins organically with small errands and snowballs into full-time caregiving.

Physical Burnout: Parents with cognitive decline, like dementia or chronic pain, may exhibit behavioral changes, confusion, or agitation, which are highly stressful to manage. And, hands-on tasks such as bathing, dressing, medication management, and mobility assistance require immense physical energy, often leading to chronic fatigue.

Financial Burdens: The cost of medical supplies, home modifications, or specialized care often falls on the adult children, which causes lost wages if they must reduce their work hours to provide care.

Family Conflict: Often, the burden of care falls disproportionately on one sibling, which can cause intense feelings of resentment and strained family dynamics.

"The way we care for aging parents is the blueprint we leave behind for our own children to follow."

Suggestions to Assist with Care

While the role is demanding, there are ways to prevent total burnout:

- **Seek Outside Help**: Research local adult day programs, respite care, or in-home aids to share the physical workload.
- **Established Support Networks**: Join local caregiver support groups and learn about creating healthy boundaries.
- **Involve the Family**: Hold family meetings and let everyone talk about what they can and can't do. Delegate responsibilities such as finances, medical appointments, or grocery shopping so that the responsibility does not fall on one person.
- **Shared Calendars**: Use apps like TimeTree or Google Calendar to coordinate doctor appointments, grocery runs, and visits among siblings.
- **Smart Home Tech:** Install indoor cameras (with permission), Smart locks, and a medical alert button so you can monitor their safety from their own home
- **Automatic Medication Dispensers**: Used locked, timed pill dispensers that beep when it is time for a dose and text you if a dose is missing.
- **Automatic Bill Pay**: For recurring utilities and insurance from their bank account, so no critical service gets shut off.
- **Outsource Everyday Tasks:** Set up meal delivery services, rideshare for seniors, and professional house cleaning services.
- **In Home Care**: Hire home health aides for four to 8 hours a week to help with bathing, dressing, and companionship.
- **Schedule "Off" Time**: Block out specific days or weekends where another relative or paid caregiver takes over completely so you can focus entirely on your spouse and children.

"There are only four kinds of people in the world: those who have been caregivers, those who are currently caregivers, those who will be caregivers, and those who will one day need caregivers."

Absent Sibling

Sudden Inheritance Syndrome

When a parent needs care, the heavy lifting usually falls on just one or two dedicated family members, while others stay distanced to avoid the stress, cost, or emotional toll. Yet the moment the parent passes away, those same distant relatives reappear and expect an equal share of the estate.

If family members are giving up their time, career advancement, or money to care for a parent, they should not do it for free while others do nothing.

What Can Be Done?

Reduce the Inheritance Through Care Agreements

- **Personal Care Agreement**: This is a formal, legal contract between the aging parent and the caregiver relative who agrees to provide caregiver services for a disabled or aging person receiving the care.
- **How it Works:** The parent pays the caregiving child a fair market wage out of their savings and allows the caregiver to be compensated for their time and services.
- **Keep Records**: Log every dollar spent on groceries, medications, home repairs, and gas for doctor visits.
- **Prevents Family Accusations/Conflict**: When absent siblings suddenly appear, they often accuse the caregiver of "stealing" or "mismanaging" the parent's money. Having clean financial records completely shuts down these accusations and keeps the relationship transactional in a healthy, transparent way rather than secretive.

- **The Result:** This legally transfers assets to the person doing the actual work, rightfully reducing the final inheritance pool left for the relatives who did not contribute.

Elder Financial Abuse

Inheritance Impatience

When elderly or disabled parents lose their independence, some adult children experience a shift in mindset, viewing their parents as a financial asset rather than a human being who needs care.

- **Sense of Entitlement**: Children often rationalize taking or focusing on the money by thinking, "it will be mine eventually anyway," or "I deserve this for dealing with their care."
- **The "Dehumanizing" Effect of Illness**: When a parent loses cognitive function, like dementia, children may feel their "real" parent is already gone, leading them to focus on what remains – the estate.
- **Isolation:** The children stopped visiting or calling, but frequently check and ask about bank balances, property values, and wills.
- **Frugality at the Parents Expense**: Refusing to pay for quality medical care, comfortable housing, or assistive devices to "preserve" the size of the inheritance.
- **Sudden Document Changes**: Pressuring a vulnerable parent to change the power of attorney, deed, or will.

"An inheritance is a potential gift left over after a long life, not a guaranteed entitlement owed to anyone right now."

What is Undue Influence?

You fought a good fight, finished the race, and kept the faith. Take advantage of aging or vulnerable parents, which is devastatingly common. Tragically, the vast majority of elder financial exploitation is committed by family members or trusted caregivers.

When a parent's physical health or cognitive abilities decline, they become highly dependent on others, opening the door to various forms of abuse.

Awareness and recognizing the red flags early can save a vulnerable parent from severe emotional and financial devastation.

"Protect your parents health, respect their dignity, and honor their love because aging is about a life, not an inheritance."

Undue Influence is the improper use of power and pressure by a dominant person to overcome another person's free will, leading them to act against their own desires.

In a trust, undue influence occurs when someone exerts excessive pressure on a grantor to the point that it overcomes their free will and manipulates their decisions. The resulting document or action reflects the influencer's desires rather than the Grantor's true intentions, often at the expense of other rightful beneficiaries.

Undue influence is not mere persuasion, advice, or influence, but the crossing of a line where the independent judgment of the influenced party is overridden. This is usually achieved by manipulation, pressure, or exploitation of vulnerable individuals who may be pressured into signing documents, changing wills/trusts, or making financial decisions that favor the influencer.

Indicators of Undue Influence:

- Sudden and dramatic changes to estate plans.
- Unusual transactions that are contrary to the Grantor's

intentions.

- The influencer actively participates in the transaction or document preparation.
- The influencer uses tactics that are more than simple advice, including misrepresentation.
- Isolation from other family members.
- Interference in communications.
- The Grantor lacked the mental capacity to create the trust at the time it was made.

Proving undue influence can be challenging, as it often occurs behind closed doors and without obvious evidence.

If undue influence is proven in court, several remedies for consequences may follow:

- The transaction or contract may be avoided or set aside.
- Assets may be returned to their rightful owner or redistributed according to prior intentions.
- The influencer may be subject to civil liability or, in extreme cases, criminal penalties.
- Court-appointed guardians or fiduciaries may intervene to protect vulnerable parties.

Closing Thoughts

Safeguarding against undue influence requires vigilance, education, and ethical conduct from all parties involved. By recognizing its signs and understanding its consequences, individuals can better protect themselves and those vulnerable to coercion, ensuring that decisions reflect genuine intent rather than manipulation.

Work with an attorney who will provide independent advice, acting solely in the best interest of the Grantor without being influenced by others.

Things To Remember

1. The Trust Protects People, Not Just Portfolios.

- **The Living First**: A trust ensures parents are properly cared for and financially protected during their vulnerable sunset years, long before it distributes inheritance to heirs.
- **Preserves Peace:** Clear legal boundaries prevent devastating sibling rivalries, financial exploitation, and misunderstandings after a parent passes.

2. A Trust is Useless If Left Unfunded

- **Asset Transfer**: Merely signing the legal paperwork is not enough.
- **Titling Matters**: Real estate, bank accounts, and investments must be legally retitled into the name of the trust to avoid probate court.

3. Choose the Trustee by Capability, Not Complacency

- **Emotional Distance**: The Trustee should be someone with integrity, organized, reliable, and capable of handling intense family dynamics neutrally, and trusted to administer the trust according to the Grantors' wishes and not their own.
- **Co-Trustees**: Consider a neutral third-party trustee if siblings have a history of conflict or if a family member might take advantage of a weak state.

4. Treat the Trust as a Living Document

- **Regular Updates**: Life changes rapidly. Trusts must be reviewed and updated after major life events like births, deaths, divorces, or significant changes in tax laws.

- **Your Assets May Change**: If you buy property, sell investments, start a business, or gain significant new assets, your trust may need to be adjusted.
- **Trustees or Beneficiaries May No Longer Be the Best Choice:** The people you originally named may have moved on, become unable to serve, or no longer fit your intentions.
- **Capacity Checks:** Update documents while parents still possess full mental and cognitive clarity to avoid future legal challenges regarding undue influence.
- **Your Goals May Evolve:** You may want different instructions for distributions, charity gifts, long-term care planning, or support for children or other family members.

5. List Smaller Items

- **Add a Personal Property Memorandum:** A simple written list added to your trust paperwork which states who gets what for smaller items like jewelry, clothing, furniture, appliances, pictures, etc., (e.g., “gold watch to grandson Mikey).

Professional Service Providers

1. Estate Planning Attorney:

- A legal professional who specializes in helping you protect your assets while you are alive and dictates how your property and healthcare will be managed if you become incapacitated or pass away. They will draft essential documents like wills, trusts, and powers of attorney, and help minimize estate taxes.

Be Aware: While most lawyers follow strict ethical codes, there are some estate planning attorneys who look out for their own best interests by recommending complex, multi-layered trusts and charging you extra costs - ask for flat-fee pricing. Some may try to pressure you into naming them as the Trustee of your trust, which would allow them to collect lucrative statutory fees from your estate later. You decide whom to appoint as your Trustee. Do not let them keep the original trust; otherwise, your family is forced to hire them to handle your estate when you pass away – you store your original executed documents in a secure safe place. Look for an estate planning attorney who will truly prioritize your needs, customize your plan, and have transparent pricing.

2. Trust Administration Attorneys

- Guides the successor trustee through the legal and financial process of managing a trust after the Grantor passes away or becomes incapacitated. They ensure the Trustee satisfies all state laws, avoids personal liability, and correctly distributes assets to beneficiaries.

Be Aware: The opportunity for abuse or self-serving behavior is real. Some attorneys will drag out the process by delaying the distribution of assets to the beneficiaries so they can continue billing the trust for ongoing communications and meetings. They bill their high attorney hourly rate for basic clerical tasks instead of utilizing paralegals at a fraction of the cost. They claim a simple estate requires formal accounting when a simple, transparent report to beneficiaries would suffice.

Look for an attorney who will give you a comprehensive outline of exactly what needs to happen and when. One that will give you upfront cost estimates for the entire administration process, rather than an open-ended hourly agreement. And one that will actively look for ways to save the trust money by instructing you to handle simple administrative tasks. And look for an attorney who will answer your questions directly in simple language, return phone calls promptly, and encourage you to keep the beneficiaries regularly updated to prevent suspicion.

3. Certified Public Accountant (CPA):

- Files the descendants' final individual tax returns and handles the trust's fiduciary tax returns to manage any income generated by trust assets after death.

Be Aware: While the vast majority of CPAs maintain high professional standards, bad actors do exist. An unethical CPA might perform services at highly inflated rates and funnel cash into their own pockets.

4. Financial Advisor:

- Help manage, liquidate, or retitle investment portfolios, stocks, or retirement accounts held within or outside the trust.

Be Aware: Advisors with direct access to account credentials or serving as a trustee have been known for making unauthorized wire transfers out of the client's trust into personal bank accounts or may buy and sell stocks within the trust portfolio at an extreme rate to generate massive commission fees for themselves.

5. Certified Property Appraisers:

- Values real estate, businesses, and high-value personal property (like extensive jewelry or coin collections) as of the exact date of death to establish stepped-up tax bases.

Be Aware: For property, require an independent appraisal and never rely solely on a realtor's comparative market analysis. Hire an independent, licensed property appraiser to establish baseline value before interviewing agents.

6. Real Estate Agents:

- Assists the Trustee in preparing, listing, and selling any trust-owned real property if the trust dictates that the home should be sold rather than transferred to a beneficiary. The agent owes the Trustee strict fiduciary duties, which are the highest standards of care and loyalty implied by law. The agent's job is not just to find a buyer but to legally protect the Trustee, who is personally vulnerable to lawsuits from the trust's beneficiaries if the sale goes wrong. The agent must place the financial interest of the trust entirely above their own or anyone else's.

Be Aware: In a trust and estate situation, there can be crooked and unethical realtors who actively target and exploit grieving families, out-of-town trustees, and vulnerable elderly individuals who may not understand the true market value of their properties. The agent can convince an uneducated trustee to sell the home "off market" quickly for cash. The agent deliberately suggests listing the home drastically below market value, telling you it "needs too much work" and sells to their own investor partner. The investor flips it weeks later for a massive profit, and the agent collects a double commission and, in some cases, offers kickbacks. An agent may also try to represent both the trust (the seller) and the buyer. They will manipulate the price downward to ensure the buyer gets a deal, prioritizing their whole double commission over the trust's financial health and often causing the trust to lose tens of thousands of dollars.

Interview at least three realtors and ask for their experience with trust and probate sales. Look for a realtor with proven experience in probate **and trust sales. Require in writing that the property must be listed at least 5 to 7 days before the Trustee accepts any offer. This ensures fair** market value. The trust should explicitly state that any real estate sales must require an independent, certified appraisal first. This blocks dishonest agents from selling family properties under market value to their cronies.

7. Probate Attorney (If Necessary):

- Probate Attorneys legally guide trustees, administrators, and beneficiaries through the court-supervised legal process of settling a deceased person's estate. The probate attorney's primary job is to act as a legal shield, ensuring the Trustee administers the estate correctly so they are never held personally liable for a breach of duty, and that the Trustee acts in the absolute best interest of the beneficiaries.

Be Aware: Rather than focus on the well-being of the Trustee or beneficiaries, there are some probate attorneys who will act unethically and illegally. While the law strictly regulates "ordinary" probate fees, self-serving attorneys find ways to bypass these limits to maximize their own payouts, like billing excessive, unjustified fees or encouraging unnecessary probate court battles to drive up legal costs. Since some successor trustees are often grieving family members who do not know probate law, attorneys will exploit the trustees' lack of knowledge by overcharging the trust to perform unnecessary legal tasks, knowing the Trustee will blindly approve the invoices from the trust funds.

The attorneys will also weaponize family conflicts by fueling beneficiary disputes. Instead of helping the Trustee mediate minor disagreements among siblings or heirs, an unethical attorney may escalate tensions; more conflict means more letters, more phone calls, and significantly higher billable hours. In some cases, attorneys might turn a blind eye when the Trustee improperly and illegally siphons money from the estate, or refuse to provide transparent, court-required accountings or actively hides receipts and transaction records from beneficiaries.

Trustees should look for an attorney who specializes in trust and estate law, offers clear hourly rates or flat fees, one who will explain things in simple, everyday words, has a track record in navigating family dynamics, has a clean professional record, and makes sure they have the time to answer your calls.

8. Probate Court/Judges

- Probate court and judges have a legal obligation to protect the "intent of the person who created the trust" and to act as an impartial finder of fact and law to ensure the trust is being administered honestly and exactly as the creator intended. The judge's core duty is to evaluate the evidence presented, interpret the trust document, and issue binding orders to protect the estate from mismanagement or fraud.

Be Aware: The court system is not completely immune to illegal influence. Probate loops often feature a small, tight-knit circle of judges, local estate attorneys, and court-appointed guardians who work together daily. This familiarity can sometimes lead to favoritism or rubber stamping.

In Conclusion

When working with professional service providers, vet them carefully. Ask for upfront fee estimates in writing, review every single billable line item before paying it, and never assume a professional is right just because they have a license.

Make sure your trust is a well-worded, solid trust that is kept updated so the court does not take you or your family's time, money, sanity, and privacy.

Do everything you can to avoid probate. It can become a machine that sometimes involves bad actors who find their way to excessively bill, purposely delay, and self-deal.

The emotional strain of settling an estate, combined with the significant sums of money involved, can create opportunities for misconduct and fraudulent practices amongst service providers and legal professionals. This is one of the gravest ethical and systematic violations that can be committed.

"A clear plan protects your wealth from the system. By managing the legal process correctly today, we ensure the courts never get a vote in our family's tomorrow."

Avoid Probate Altogether

Establish a well-worded, solid trust, and keep it updated so the court does not take you or your family's time, money, sanity, and privacy.

"The legal process is temporary, but the family legacy you are protecting is forever."

Final Conclusion

Ask yourself, "What will life be like for my family when I'm gone?" and prepare accordingly.

A living trust is not just a legal document but a profound act of love and responsibility that protects your legacy and spares your family from the stress of probate. Creating a trust takes effort today, but the true value is the Peace of Mind that it provides, ensuring that your wishes are honored and that your loved ones are cared for when it matters most.

www.ingramcontent.com/pod-product-compliance
Lightning Source LLC
LaVergne TN
LVHW070247220926
848482LV00034B/509
* 9 7 9 8 2 9 5 4 4 2 8 4 1 *